Prayers for Young People

DAVID GATWARD

Lord, I'm in Love! (I Think)

First published in 1996 by
KEVIN MAYHEW LTD
Rattlesden
Bury St Edmunds
Suffolk IP30 0SZ

© 1996 Kevin Mayhew Ltd

The right of David Gatward to be identified as the author
of this work has been asserted by him in accordance with
the Copyright, Designs and Patents Act 1988.

All rights reserved. No part of this publication may be
reproduced, stored in a retrieval system, or transmitted,
in any form or by any means, electronic, mechanical,
photocopying, recording or otherwise, without the
prior written permission of the publisher.

ISBN 0 86209 827 0
Catalogue No 1500064

0 1 2 3 4 5 6 7 8 9

Cover illustration by Roy Mitchell

Design by Veronica Ward
Artwork Graham Johnstone

Edited by Peter Dainty
Typesetting by Louise Hill
Printed and bound in Great Britain

Contents

Lord, Can We Talk?	5
Alone	8
Boy Meets Girl	10
Sex!!	13
Love	17
All I Offered	20
Hey, Good Lookin'!	25
Just Admiring!	30

Lord, Can We Talk?

Lord, can we talk?
I feel daft praying about this again
　　but I feel I've got no one else to talk to –
　　just you.
It's girls again!
That time-old problem.
What am I going to do, Lord?
I'm so confused.
It's so painful knowing
　　what I could do if I were home.
But I'm not!
I'm here,
　　a hundred miles away from
　　a very special person.
It's not fair, God!
Remember her letter?
And how about when we said
　　'goodbye'?
'Go and find someone good enough
　　for you,' she said.
For goodness sake –
　　I was saying goodbye to her!
The person good enough for me;
　　now gone!

She hasn't even written.
Can't blame her really,
   after my last letter,
     and knowing now how I feel.

My God. Why?
Come on, Lord, would you write?
I gave her no choice I guess;
   went out on my own
     before consulting you.
But I love her! (At least I think I do!)
What I'd do given half the chance.
If only I knew how to make her love me.
But I don't.
And even if I did, no use it'd be,
   being here.
I'm a victim of geography.
I've lost again, God,
   I've lost again!
And I don't know what to do;
   I daren't write,
   I daren't 'phone.
I'm so screwed up.
What chance is there for anything
   with a hundred mile gap?
All through the others

I knew deep down
how I really felt,
yet I had to spend two years,
    helping her through!
Holding myself back from reaching out.

Lord, you know how I really fell for her.
Good grief,
    even mum and dad could tell!
'Hang in there,' I get told.
'It depends how much you want her.'
But, Lord, all I can do is sit and cry!
    cry about a friendship;
    one that became the centre of my life,
    one I so wanted to develop
    into something more.
It was never given a chance.
But even though I *may*
    have lost a girlfriend
    (and the *may* is in your hands, Lord!),
    I gained the greatest, most caring,
    understanding, and lovely person
    as a friend.
Thank you, Lord.

Amen.

Alone

Lord, can't you hear me?
Don't you hear my cry of pain?
Are you there, in the darkness?
Don't you know the way I feel?

David, I am here!

Lord, I am lost, can't you find me?
I'm knocking, Lord,
   why won't you answer?
I'm alone, Lord,
   why won't you comfort me?
I'm hurt, why won't you heal?

David, I am here!

Lord, I don't know which way to turn.
I'm alone, lost, and confused.
The love I seek is gone.
Where are you, Lord?

David, I am here!

Help me, Lord!
The darkness it surrounds me!
I scrabble in the dust, alone on my knees.
My heart has been pierced,
   and my love rejected.
My life seems in ruins.
Won't you help me?

>   *David, I am here!*
>
> *My hand is outstretched for you!*
> *I love you and will never leave you!*
> *Why won't you listen?*
> *Why won't you trust?*
> *How weak your faith is!*
>
>   *I am here!*

Lord??
Is that you??

Amen.

Boy Meets Girl

Lord, are you there?
Have you got time for a chat?
Well, I just need to talk;
   talk about a problem.
It's not just mine though.
I guess all teenagers (and adults!)
   find it hard;
   the dreaded first date,
   the first kiss . . .
Lord, why is it so hard?
And not just the first time,
   but every time?
How do you approach them?
How do you let them know
   you're interested
   without coming on too strong?
How do you know
   if they're interested in you?
And why does it seem easier
   for everyone other than me?!
Good grief, Lord, take it from me,
   this boy/girl stuff is agony!
One minute you're in love,
   next minute you hate each other!

Then, you just about get it together,
   and suddenly you've left home,
   and there's no chance!

Isn't it strange
   how this person seems to be
   the one for you,
   without whom you'd die
   of a broken heart,
   unable to go on!
Couldn't you make it easier, Lord?
You know, actually *tell* us if it is
   the right one,
   or if we actually stand a chance?
It's all so hit and miss.
   (I'm not the only one who
   feels like this, am I, Lord?)

I know I'm asking a bit too much,
   and I'm sorry.
If I'm honest I have to admit
   that even though a lot of pain
   and heartache is involved,
   it's still exciting!
In fact a lot of it is good fun!
When it does work out,

even for a short time,
it's fantastic!

Lord, thank you for giving me
   the ability to survive
   the turmoils of teenage love.
Give me the courage and strength
   to keep going.
Help me to get better at this
   'game of love'.
Finally, Lord, I pray
   that when I do find 'the one',
   you will be there to keep us together,
   and to help it last.

Amen.

SEX!!

Lord, can we talk?
It's about SEX.
The three-letter word,
 abused by some,
 loved by others,
 the subject of jokes,
 the cause of giggling
 in a class of eleven year olds,
 even the cause of embarrassment.
All due to one word.

What is it about that small word
 that scares people?
It brings them out in a cold sweat!
They stutter, go red;
 all due to that one word.
To be honest, Lord, so do I.
The trouble is, is that, well, er . . .
 actually, Lord, what is the trouble?
Everyone is either male or female,
 their sex.
To produce offspring,
 all species have sex.
Couples use sex as a way of expressing

their love for one another.
There, all wrapped up, neat and tidy.
But it's not that easy, Lord, is it?

Sex is a problem.
First, and most important for me,
　is the 'pre-marital sex' problem.
Lord, I really understand why people
　sleep with each other.
When the lights are low, the music soft,
　the two of you are on your own,
　it's hard to say 'no'.

So many people do it.
So many of my friends do it.
It seems to be a part of life,
　completely natural.
But if only they knew.
Lord, sex is a gift from you.
And it's not given for the cheap thrill.

Lord, I'd be a liar if I said I'd never
　wanted to sleep with someone.
Of course I have.
Everyone has or will do.
We're only human.

The sexual urge is natural, normal.
It's controlling it that's the problem!
If only people were more open,
    more willing to understand.
Many my age think,
'Well, I've done it now, so why stop?'

There's only one reason, Lord:
    I want to save myself for
    that one special person.
I don't want to be there, and say,
    'You're the twentieth person
    I've slept with.'
I want to give that person all of me.
But that's me, Lord.
Where does that leave
    those that have
    slept around a bit,
    those that feel it's too late?
They've spoilt something precious,
    and irreplaceable,
    and now can't be forgiven?
Please, Lord, tell them.
Tell them they're not alone,
    that you understand,
    and that they are forgiven.

16 SEX!!

Help us all, Lord,
   to come to terms with sex;
   not to shy away from it,
   not to give in.
But to realise how important
   and beautiful it is.
To remember how fragile it is.
Never to forget it is your gift to us.

Amen.

Love

Lord, it's about 'love'.
That word, that wonderful four letter word.
Did you ever realise that it would
   hold so much power?
Have so many meanings?
Can we just think about it
   for a moment, Lord?
Because I have to admit
   that I find it all rather confusing.

LOVE
What is it, Lord?
What does it mean?
For it's used in so many different ways,
   each one almost contradicting the others.
How many people say 'I love'
   without realising the full
   potential of that word?
For example, Lord,
   I love chocolate,
   and I also love music,
   and going to the theatre.
Yet at the same time I also love my family,
   I love my friends,

I love you!
You see?
I use the same word but to mean
   something different each time!
I can hardly compare my love of chocolate
   with the love I have for my family!

And then also, Lord, I can think
   of other situations:
   when, 'I love you' is whispered
   into a loved one's ear,
   or you 'make love' with your partner.
(Now there's an interesting thought, Lord!)
How do you make love?
Are there special ingredients?
'Leave for 1-2 hours in the oven,
   until brown on top'!

Quite humorous don't you think, Lord?
But maybe not so far from the truth.
You know, Lord,
   I think there are special ingredients
   that make for real love.

Remember that passage from
   the Bible, Lord?

Love is very patient and kind, never jealous or envious, never boastful or proud, never haughty or selfish or rude. Love does not demand its own way. It is not irritable or touchy. It does not hold grudges, and will hardly even notice when others do it wrong. It is never glad about injustice, but rejoices whenever truth wins out. If you love someone you will be loyal to them no matter what the cost. You will always believe in them, always expect the best of them, and always stand your ground in defending them.

I Corinthians 13:4-7

The ingredients of love.
A long recipe for such a small word!

But just as a final request, Lord,
    teach me to love;
    to love the way you love
    each and every one of us,
    no matter what we do.
And above all, Lord,
    help me to love you.

Amen.

ALL I OFFERED

This prayer gives me a very strange feeling as I read it again. I wrote it in the November of my 'A Level' year at Sixth Form College. It was a time in my life when I didn't really know what was happening to me. I'd messed up my mocks the year before and was therefore having to work twice as hard. I was in a local rock band and we had started doing a few gigs and were practising hard. And in the middle of all this there was me – confused, screwed up and depressed.

You only have to look at some of the prayers that I wrote at the time and that appear in *Can We Talk, Lord?* to realise the state I'd got myself into. Reading them now, I realise how I was often worrying unduly, and frequently getting over-anxious about things that ultimately don't matter very much. Yet at the time I really was confused and emotionally and spiritually depressed. And the reason? I'm still trying to figure that one out! One problem I can put my finger on was the loneliness I felt at the time. I wanted someone to confide in, a friend to talk to, share with, depend on. Knowing that, you can probably imagine how I felt when after giving a friend a birthday present they just handed it back to me and walked away.

That incident really brought home to me how much I needed friendship and yet also how vulnerable it makes us. I know it's only too easy to sit back and with a toothpaste-bright 'Jesus loves me'-smile to say, 'I only need the Lord'. Now this may be true, but I believe there's more to it than that. I look at the Gospels and find that Jesus needed friends. He needed those he could talk to, confide in, have a good laugh with. He needed them, and yet as I read on and find myself in the Garden of Gethsemane with Jesus and those same friends, I find they let him down. They went to sleep, they ignored his pain, and he found that all he had left was his Father. And that's what I found – when all else fails he is still there, waiting open-armed to hold you close. Jesus knows how good it is to have friends, and also how it hurts when they let you down and leave you alone. So who better to talk to when that's where you are – left on your own?

Lord, don't you care?
So many times I've come to you for help,
 yet I hear no answer.
So many times I've needed comfort,
 yet there is none.
So many times I've put my trust in you,
 and wondered why.
Why me?
Why is it always me?
I know my problems are small
 compared to others;
 but to me?
To me they are heartbreaking.
It's so easy to say, 'Trust in Jesus!'
But how can I, when it seems
 to make no difference?
What are you playing at?
Are you testing me?
Why, Lord?
What have I done?
Is there any purpose to it?
Whenever things start going right,
 something happens,
 and I'm down again;
 down in the dirt,
 alone on my knees;

my fingers and hands
cut and bleeding
as I try desperately
to pull myself up
and start again.
But there is no rest,
   no peace.

Do you know what it's like to have
   friendship thrown back in your face?
All I offered was a gift.
Nothing special.
Just something to bring a smile.

But it wasn't accepted.
A slap on the cheek.
It hurt, Lord.
Something so small, yet it hurt.
I could have cried.

But again, no one was there.

Lord?

Come to me, please.
I've kept on fighting.

But now?
Now I don't know.
It's as if I'm always alone;
   alone again,
   to face things as one solitary heart,
   standing in the rain
   as the crowds rush by.
Not a glance, Lord.
Not one
   caring,
   fleeting,
   glance.

'David, my son,
   I know what it's like.
Believe me, I've been there.
All I needed was a helping hand,
   the shoulder of a friend.
But they were asleep, David.
They were asleep.
I died for them, David.
I died for you.'

Amen.

Hey, Good Lookin'!

Every morning when I have to get up and look at myself in the mirror the thought that immediately enters my mind is a combination of 'Urgh!' and 'Help!' The reflection that stares at me through bleary eyes bears a distinct likeness to Cro-Magnon Man – stubbled chin, knotted unkempt hair, dull unintelligent eyes.

It's all there. Even as I surface into something akin to consciousness it doesn't appear any better. Through eyes that are trying to get used to the idea of being awake and are showing a distinct lack of interest I note that my chin has a marked similarity to a badly sown lawn, through which zits are doing their best to turn it into a scale model of a moonscape. A quick wash makes some difference, but it still doesn't stop me from believing that I look hideous.

Like most lads, I'd like to think that I was God's gift to the opposite sex – but that mirror daily reminds me that I'm not! And the closer I look at me, the less I like what I see. (Hey, that rhymes!) The trouble is, society emphasises the importance of appearance. Dress sense, a good physique, how you present yourself, your 'image', these are all so important. If you don't 'look right' you might as well give up! Fortunately God isn't so short-sighted – he's more interested in what we're like inside. I know that that can often be like glimpsing into the depths of a disgusting dustbin, but at least what's inside can be cleaned up and transformed by the power of his love.

With all our yukiness, grime and filth, he still loves us, and wants to change us. He sees what we are, and also what we can be. So, next time you look in the mirror and you see 'spot city' staring back – smile! God sees inside, and he loves the person he sees and what that person can become with his help!

Lord, why am I so ugly?
Every time I look in the mirror
　I want to hide away,
　or maybe even die!
Everyone seems so much more
　attractive than me!
I've worse acne for a start!
Now, there's a point, Lord;
　why did you create acne?
Is it a sadistic joke?

something to tickle the ribs
of the heavenly host?
Well, Lord,
  it's not funny!
I don't enjoy waking in the morning
  and looking at something
  resembling a pizza!
Nothing gets rid of them,
  not even surgical spirits!
  (And believe me, I've tried!)
And then, Lord, there's the rest of me.
My ears are too big.
And my nose!
  Now *there's* a subject
  for conversation.
Lord, they could use this
  to model a ski-jump on!
  It's huge!
We've gone beyond Pinocchio,
  and we're into elephant country here!
And what about the fact
  that my whole body seems to be
  strangely mis-shaped,
  perhaps even deformed!
Too thin, and yet too fat
  at the same time!

And my feet!
>   We're talking about battleships here
>   and verging onto aircraft carriers!
Then finally,
>   there's my hair.
Walk down the street
>   and what do you see?
Nice hair,
>   in good condition,
>   stays in style . . .
Then there's mine!
>   I've come to the conclusion
>   that my hair is alive,
>   and none too pleased
>   with the experience.
I look like a walking haystack!
'Oh, it can look great . . .
>   for five minutes after combing.
Then it's a mess
>   and even a blow dry doesn't tame it.
AAAAAARRRRRGGGHH!!!!
Lord, I'm sorry for being so ungrateful.
You created me,
>   and in your eyes I'm beautiful
>   (even if it's only you and my mum
>   that thinks so!)

Help me to be satisfied.
I'm so lucky compared to some,
    yet I forget and get wrapped-up
    in having to 'look good'.

Help me to be more concerned about
    the 'inner me'.
And to stop hiding behind
    a false self-made 'image'.
Teach me, Lord,
    that it's not what's on the outside
    that counts,
    but that which is within,
    the image that is of the Creator.

Amen.

Just Admiring!

Lord,
I'm sitting in a lecture and I'm not listening.
Neither am I taking part in 'group discussion',
 'note taking' or 'question answering'.
I am not sharpening my pencil, underlining a
 title or thinking that I need to ask the
 lecturer a question.

No, Lord.
My mind is elsewhere.
As are my eyes.

You see, Lord,
 sitting in a room with two hundred other
 students allows you certain advantages.
And I'm making full use of them, Lord.
One could almost say that I am
 admiring your artwork,
 enjoying your masterly creation,
 soaking up the heady atmosphere
 as I gorge my soul upon the sights
 of silent beauty before my eyes.
One could also say that I am girl watching,
 checking out the talent or ogling!

JUST ADMIRING 31

Call it what you will, but I'm doing exactly
   that and loving it!
Hip hip hurrah! for yet another one of
   your great ideas – attraction!
I'm sure I am not the only enthusiast –
   even in this room!
Sitting in the silent privacy afforded by a
   lecture presents a perfect hide of
   camouflage!
Armed with only your eyes the hours can
   seem to just whizz by as new details
   flutter into sight!

And it's the little details that count.

You see, Lord, in a lecture you can be
   pretty much on your own.
Unlike being out with friends where the
   company often results in loud 'Fwars!'
   and elaborate scoring systems,
   being on your own lets you take in the
   more intricate details.
You have more time to watch, observe –
   the way someone (that girl over there
   with the straight jet black hair)
   sits slightly forward,

chin resting on her hand,
chewing slightly the end of a pencil;
that wonderful way some hide
behind a curtain of hair,
doodling on the note pads;
those two in the corner, whispering.

Now, Lord, I'm not being disrespectful,
or sexist.
I'm just doing what people have done
throughout history, man and woman alike;
from the days of Adam
to the days of fast food,
looking and loving from afar,
not getting involved, just admiring.

And I thank you for it, Lord;
for giving us the pleasure of each other,
for the pleasure of just looking,
for the joy in just innocently watching.

. . . and especially for that girl over there
staring at the wall!

Amen.